A POETIC LIFE

A POETIC LIFE

"Meaningful Moments of Time"

Angela Duffield

Rev. date: 03/21/2017

To order additional copies of this book, contact:
Xlibris
1-888-795-4274
www.Xlibris.com
Orders@Xlibris.com
707492

CONTENTS

Amore

Number one that I bared
There came a second to be shared
Third time was a charm
Even with four there'd be no harm
Then one more to be adored
The best gifts from above, *amore!*

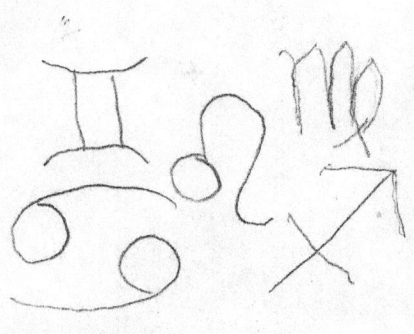

<u>Blissfulness</u>

Like the sun hot and bright
And the moon shining at night
Seeing stars in each other's eyes
Our bodies fully unite . . . *eclipse*

Thoughts of you and me together
Becoming one let's do whatever
It may be as best friends/lovers
Unconditionally forever

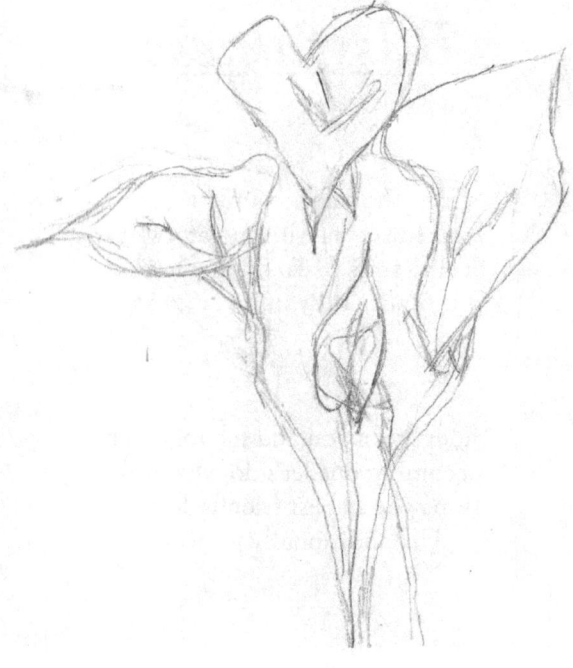

Y'all know the quote
If you love someone let them go,
And if they come back they're yours forever
Well, it seems when I love and let go
They come back whenever
So this is my quote
Love each other, let go and come back together;
If it's at the same time, it's meant to be forever.

The mentality of love and life is within you
Your faith, friends, family, surroundings
Your emotions, dreams and wishes too
All a journey from your originality to your destiny
Like magnets, we are meant to attract
So hold tight, have no regret
And absolute is what you'll get

Choices

You can do anything
Have whatever you want, if given or bought
Try to make good *choices*
And remember what you were taught
Each of you make a difference in life through love
Don't believe anyone that tells you
That you were never thought of

So much to say, but can't
Either say it or don't
Down on paper write it
Either will or won't
Neither speechless or illiterate
Just don't give up, let go, or quit

Just Imagine

Just imagine being betrayed by family and friends
Having to meet new people, who to trust
I'm sure you've been betrayed by the ones you love
For the ones who haven't *just imagine*
Having to do almost everything on your own
To have children that see you go through that
Even if it's for a short period of time
And time goes by, oh so quickly, *just imagine*
How things and people change throughout the years
The environment, the community, society
Those things affect you and your children
Just imagine and believe it's all going to be OK
Need to trust again anyway

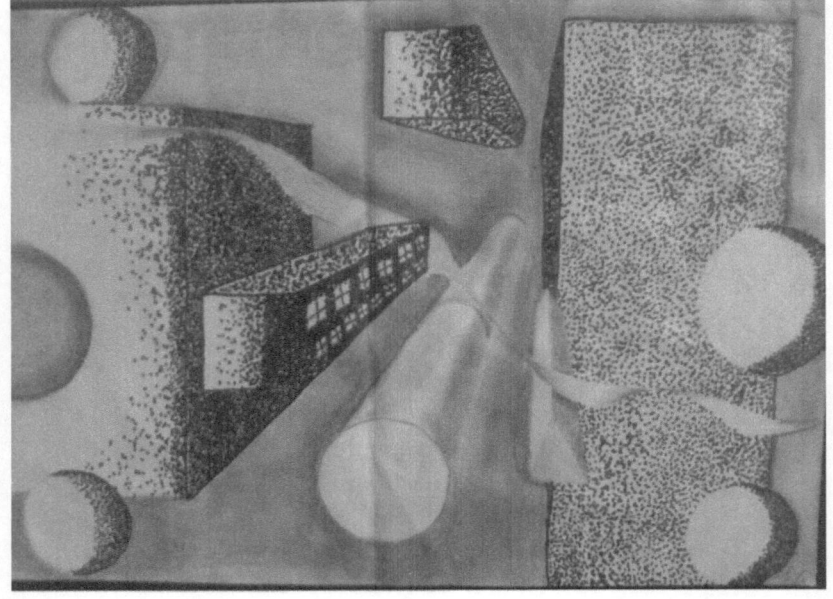

Live Game

Men and women say each lies
Naturally we change our minds
But if playing games, watch who you blame
We're responsible for our own, there's no need to disown
Learn the difference between a lie and a game
And whether a part, or just a play
If you think you can't trust me,
Think twice and use hindsight
I got intuition, you're your own vice

I keep you off my mind
Until I'm in yours to miss
That is what I do to be in my own bliss
Sometimes I don't understand
I'm not used to this
If hurting me is your bliss
Take some time to think it over
It's you I've had the best times with
Look around, read between the lines
You'll know when you find a clover
I can never hide, me, love always finds

Ever been mistaken for somebody else
Rejected and then blame yourself
Done nothing wrong but been at fault
Want to say sorry for something done when younger
And didn't get the chance to do so as an adult
If ever involved with me, my apologies to you
For any mishap, hurt, harm or mislead

Someone beautiful, yet so insecure
Told to be rich, but really poor
Wanted by people sometimes looking to score
And when around, it must take a wiz
Because I don't know what for
Neither an alcoholic, druggie, slut, or whore
But no matter what it is
Because of loving you, I forgive

When you care about others, and they do you wrong
Really they're jealous, and can't compare all along
When you think you're alone and have no one
If life's a game, try to have fun
From within feel no spite
And when you know you've done right
If the wrong comes to fight
Just be careful and don't play
You're never alone night or day

Don't think you understand when you don't
Just think I want to be around you, but I won't
If I'm alone and someone you've got
Don't think I'm not glad if you're happy, and I'm not
Don't say something if you really don't know
Say what you mean, can do, or want
Just say so and be blunt
I don't know or being unsure
Is better than lying or being hurt
If you've been through what I have
Or going through what I am
It's hard to be mad at myself or you
Remember I'm a woman, not a man

Paradise Remains

With so many strings
It's hard to break ties
All these feelings knotted up inside
How does an angel on earth fly
With broken wings to paradise

All these thoughts inside my head
Faith, hope, love, and the dead
Saints and kings, it seems they're falling apart
I'm grateful for God the Father, Jesus Christ
Constellations, astronomy, elements and art
Energy, life, intelligence, sun, moon, and stars
Integrity, values, morals, earth, and trade
They somehow never seem to fade
Chemistry, physics, science, and facts
Skill, origin, remedy, and friction
Humility, clarity, valor, and craft
It's really cool they're all nonfiction
And that my story will no longer lack

God created the world with beautiful seas, mountains
Trees, rivers, lakes, and springs
Man built a house out of dirt, water, and sticks
Woman made it home with love and dreams
Dirt became mortar, sticks became logs, and bricks
Some people built walls
But across bridges they walk
She gathers flowers, he gets supplies
They laugh, dance, sing, and talk
With a joyful heart, enchanting way, and smile
When seen together resembles paradise all the while

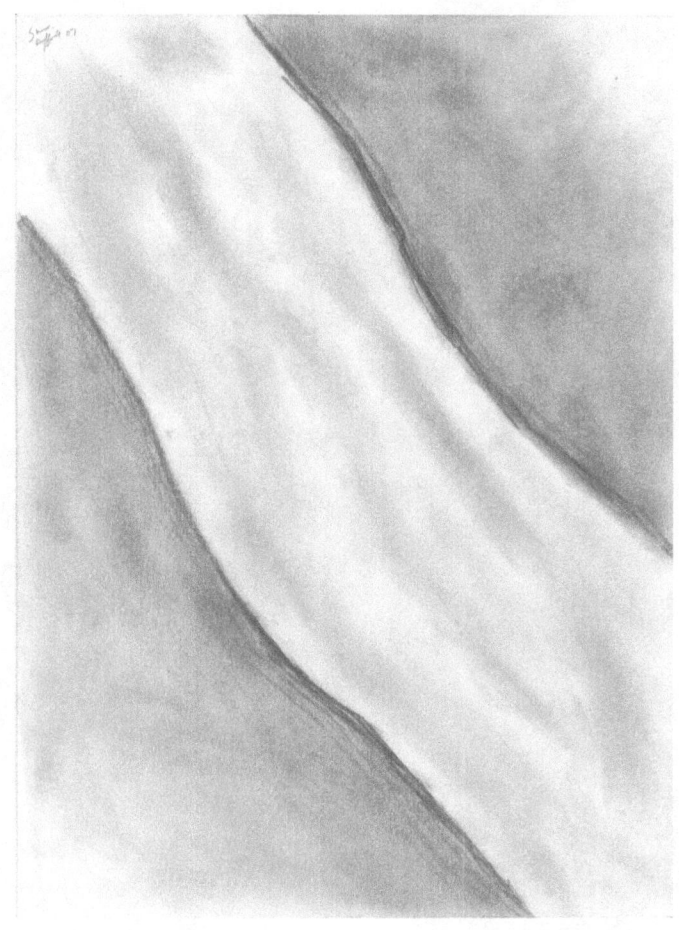

<u>Real Tales</u>

Didn't know my dad, but grew up with a faithful mother
Didn't have sisters, but five older brothers
Felt like a slave, emotionally or physically abused everyday
Only wanting to get away
Usually had somewhere else to stay
With friends, you know, that liked to play
Went away for awhile
Came back and it was like girl gone wild *(not as seen on TV)*
Everything seemed the same
Just more fun being older and part of the game
A teenager and pretty too, wishing for things that sometimes came true
Fallen in and out of love, broken hearts are what became of
Mistakes made and lessons learned too
Forgiveness and healing helped with forgetting a few
With beauty on skin and Holy Spirit within
This angel with five cherubs flies on a whim

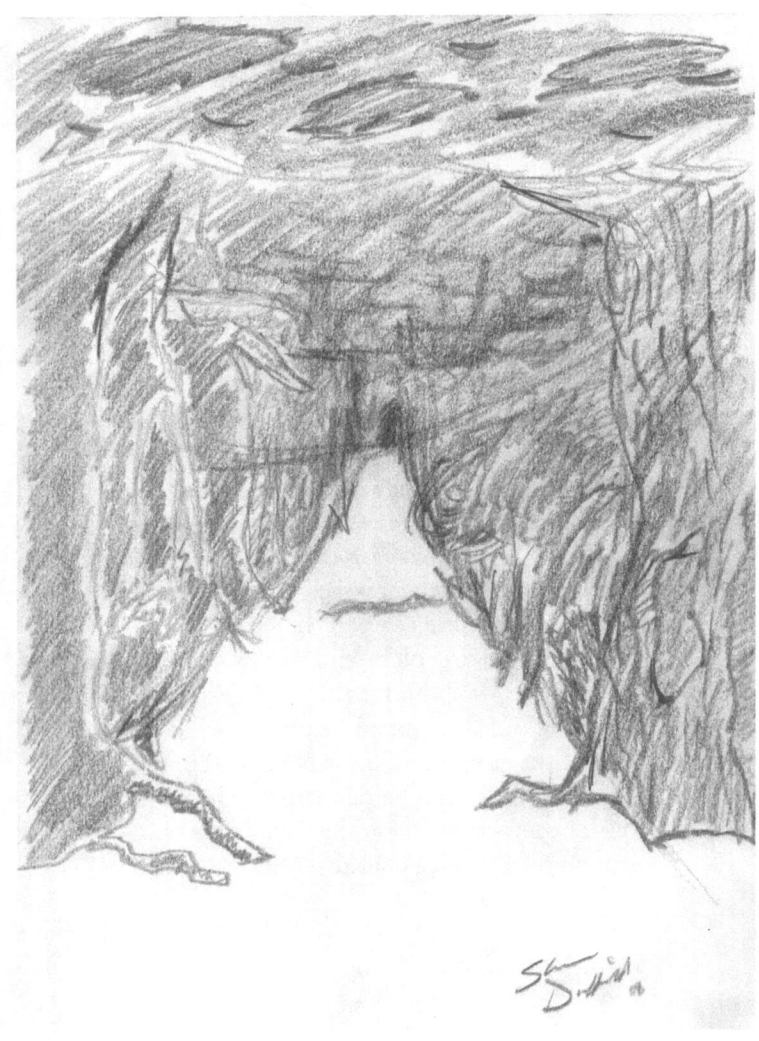

You know who, done came outta the woods
But she's good, not everyone's been through the same S—
Felt the same or been fortunate
Everybody has em', dreams I'm talkin'
All u gotta do is pick the ones to walk in
To all the good fellas
There's only one Cinderella
Oh, you want a mermaid outta the sea
Swan princess or Snow White
Nah, you don't wanna drown or freeze
Wait a minute let's go back in time, Pocahontas saved a life
What do I want? Maybe it's a fairytale need
It's never too late for happily ever after, right?
Already been through supernatural/paranormal activities
It's not all bad going through this maze
Even if it's in a haze
Years go by and I'm still sane

I've been told
I don't look my age
I'm not old
I'm going to get what I deserve
I believe in blessings, magic, luck and curse
Everyone has a plan
Help me make a stand
I don't change
I'm subject to
I think too much
My mentality is as such

I dreamt of you before we met
The city lights went out in sequence
I found my daughter, a' last you backed up
We jumped in your truck, safe and sound
In reality, you and I were together that *fall!*
We even exchanged gifts when Christmas came round
You gave me a portable charger and some books
The light on that charger, I have no control over
It just comes on and goes off whenever
I gave you a flashlight with a magnetic tip
You said you were in love with me
But got engaged to someone else
You should have been the one to tell me
That with you, our time together was a *trip*!
Not like the one before
I dreamt of you after we'd met
I don't know what for
Or if/when I'll ever see you again
But I believed everything you told me
And you took advantage of my vulnerability
I know what each of our times together meant

I lie awake at night and pray
Hope you might stop by and say
I am here so don't be sad
Let's hold each other
And relive the moments we've had

The moon was out, stars in the sky
New Year's Eve, so cold outside
No snow on the ground
Said you thought about coming to see me
Guess I'm not as important to you
As you are to me
I cried and had some rum and wine
Played games, had food, listened to music and wind chimes

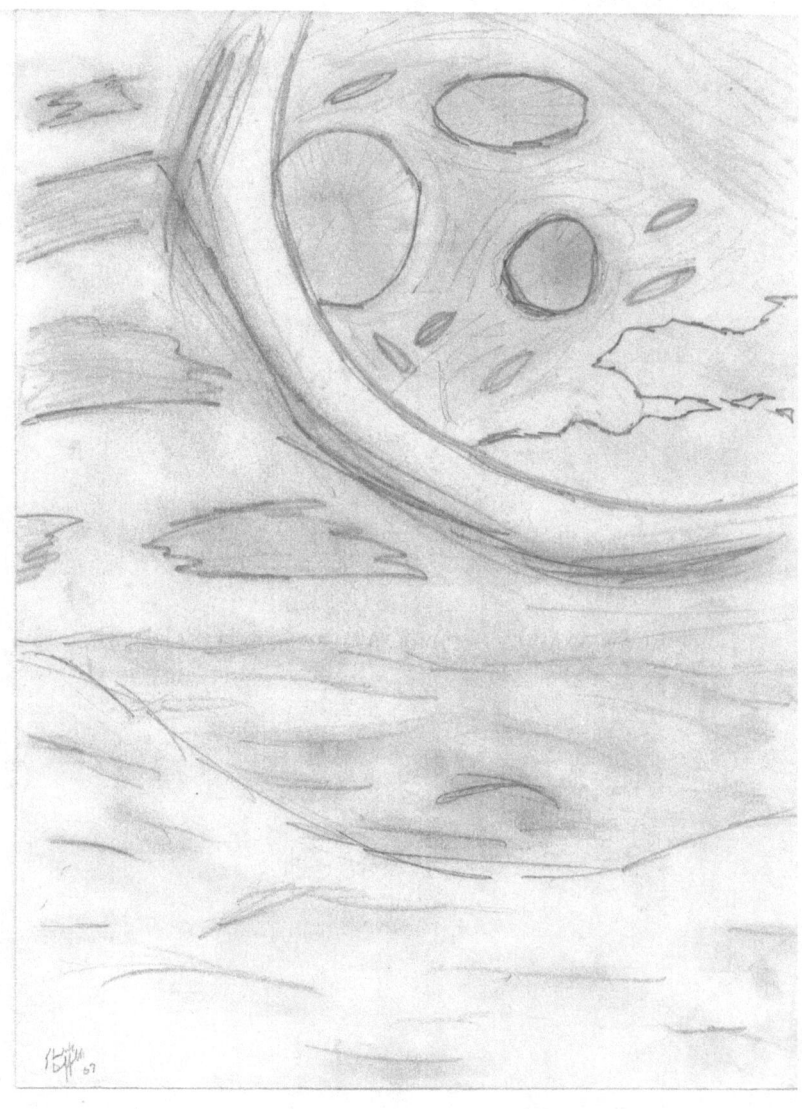

<u>*Symbolic*</u>

Broken mirror, huge cricket on shoulder
Woke up early one morn
A cat banging a bird at my door
Left apt. a day or so later
That bird brought back . . . de-feathered
Pine trees and crows, you sitting on a big rock
Writings and drawings on bathroom stalls
Tales of being marked, stalked, and then cut off
Once wiped a table clean
Son brought a feather home
The wind took it away, and he screamed

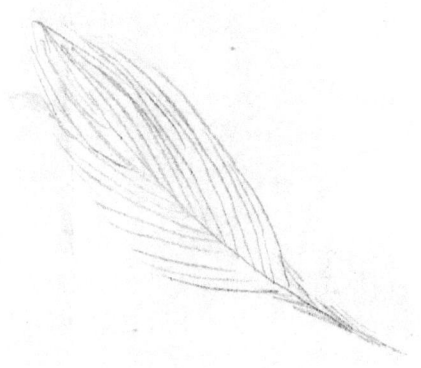

After midnight, freezing cold
Whole body soar, could barely move
But had to stay bold
Another night, almost asleep
Awoke to a matrix screech
Then again, awake or dream
Possession following or taken from me

Why do I care so much?
I get my feelings and emotions mixed up
When's the point that I don't give a S—, or F—?
And money, comparison, competition, is there a premonition?
Tell me please! What and how much do you believe?
No one likes to be alone, maybe that's why you come around
It doesn't take much to convince me
If with me, you don't want to be
In different words, is that what you told me?
And when you think you've lost or won
It's not about winning or losing, you'll see
If you're playing games, I will leave you be
Why say you care? Then you leave!
I say I care about you more than you do me
I'm not lying, and you'll think of me!

Amazing things happen all the time
Only to have a witness at that point
So many things have meaning in a life
Just to understand, pray and know
A voice heard, and someone touched
And with a wave of its tail, a deer replies hello
So many words about people and things unknown

Father Time and Mother Nature
Always work it out
Human error and technology
Make wasteful time, not doubt
We all know, not everywhere has four seasons
The saying goes, everything happens for a reason
Well I think, *accidents represent a beacon*
We've heard bad things happen to good people
And good things happen to the bad
We know good and bad things happen to both, but
Patience is a virtue and karma is rad

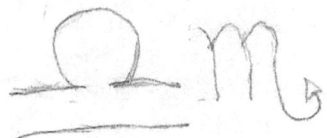

My mom was born in **September** 1943
She was **thirty-one** when she had me
At age **sixty-two** when my mom died, I was **thirty-one**
It was on my daughter's birthday in **September** 2005
I have five sisters and another brother, I found out in 2014
For **forty** years, I felt captive or quarantined
I'm glad I have a heavenly father
Some people made me feel like a bother

Is it a sign or two
There's always something
I see, hear, or do
Actually, there's been quite a few
Then someone comes into view
Were you born on a cusp too?

<u>You're</u>

I think of you when I'm alone
Where are you, do you know?
You're out there, I'm still here
But even though we are apart
You're the key to my heart

You're the love of my life,
I'll always love you more
North or South
East or West
No matter, what I'm yours

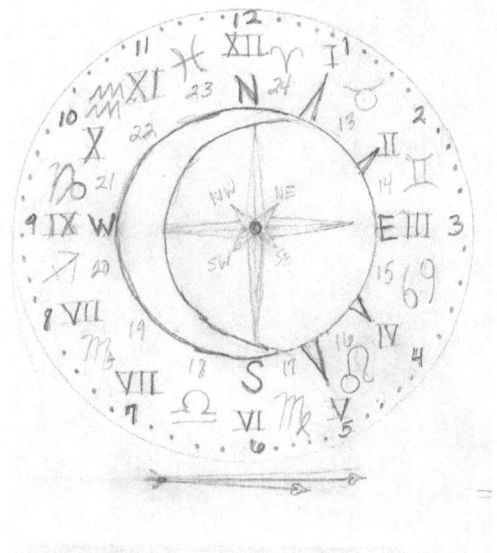

What is love?
We know it comes from up above
But what else do we know of love?
When someone says I love you
And you say I love you too
Are they sure, are you sure, is it true?
Real love may exist
Has there been or was it a miss, will there be again?
If so, true love shows and comes from within

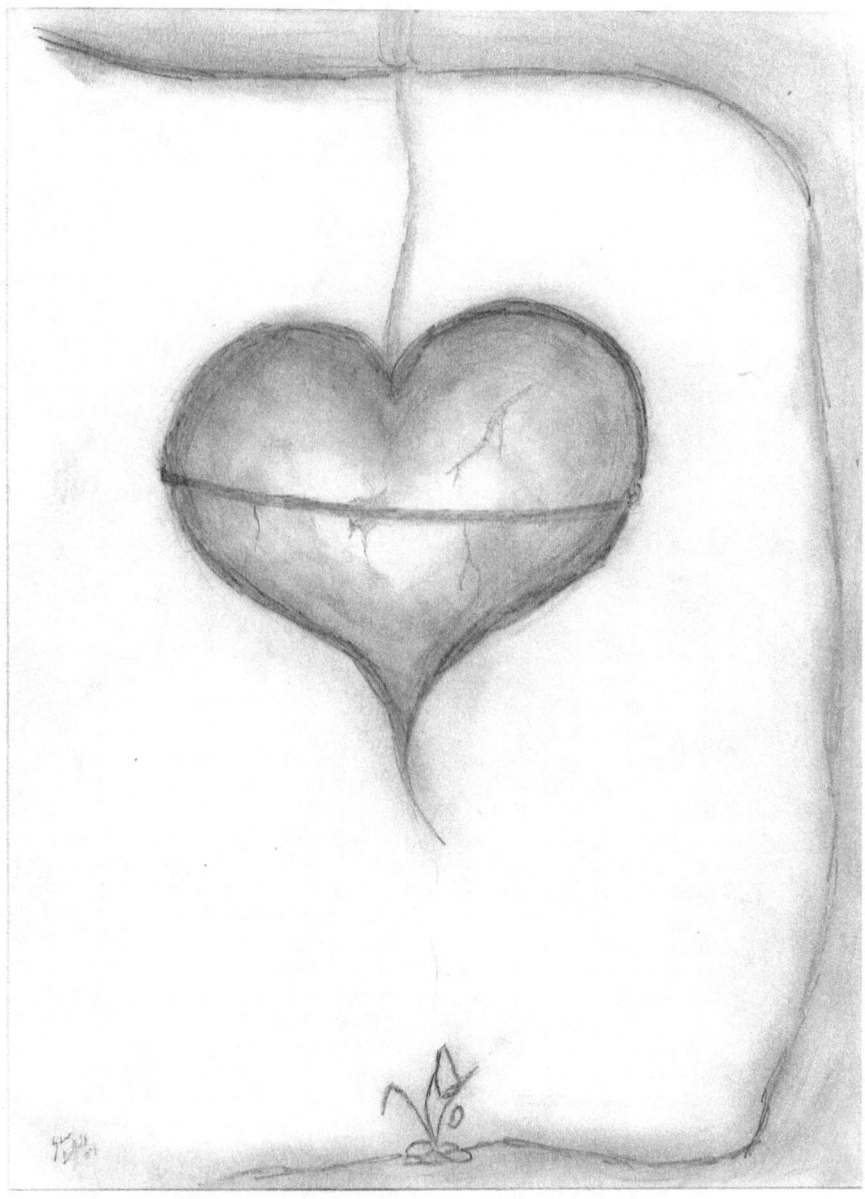

www.ingramcontent.com/pod-product-compliance
Lightning Source LLC
Chambersburg PA
CBHW021048180526
45163CB00005B/2341

* 9 7 8 1 5 1 4 4 8 3 0 9 1 *